Belly Laughs
150 Ribtickling Food Jokes

KINGFISHER
An imprint of Kingfisher Publications Plc
New Penderel House
283-288 High Holborn·
London WC1V 7HZ
www.kingfisherpub.com

First published by Kingfisher 2007
2 4 6 8 10 9 7 5 3 1

A CIP catalogue record for this book is
available from the British Library.

ISBN: 978 0 7534 1584 9

Printed in India
1TR/THOM/(PICA)/90SHES/C

Belly Laughs

150 Ribtickling Food Jokes

KINGFISHER

What happens when you tell an egg a joke?
It cracks up.

Why did the banana go to hospital?
Because it wasn't peeling very well.

What happens to a hamburger that misses a lot of school?
It has a lot of ketchup time.

**How do you turn
soup into gold?**
*Put fourteen
carrots in it.*

**Have you heard
the butter joke?**
Don't spread it.

**Why did the
monster eat a
light bulb?**
*Because he was in
need of a light
snack.*

Why did the boy push his dad into the fridge?
Because he wanted a cold pop.

What kind of crackers do firefighters like in their soup?
Firecrackers.

What do you do if a green tomato knocks on your door?
Wait until it's ripe.

"Waiter! Waiter! Will my pizza be long?"
"No, sir, it will be round."

What's the best day to eat toffees?
Chews-day.

Knock Knock!
Who's there?
Lettuce.
Lettuce who?
Lettuce in and we'll tell you!

Why do you eat so fast?
I want to eat as much as possible before losing my appetite.

Jack: Would you like some Egyptian pie?
Jill: What's Egyptian pie?
Jack: You know, the kind mummy used to make.

What did the mayonnaise say to the refrigerator?
"Shut the door, I'm dressing!"

What starts with "t" ends with "t" and is filled with "t"?
A teapot.

Why did the man eat at the bank?
He wanted to eat rich food.

What is Dracula's favourite fruit?
A neck-tarine.

Why did the priest like Swiss cheese?
Because it was hole-y.

What's Snow White's brother's name?
Egg White! Get the yolk?

What was Noah's favourite fruit?
Pears.

Why do the French eat snails?
Because they don't like fast food.

What's green and sings?
Elvis Parsley.

"Waiter! Waiter! There's a hand in my soup."
"That's not your soup, sir, it's a finger bowl."

What kind of bean doesn't grow in your garden?
A jelly bean.

Knock Knock!
Who's there?
Hammond
Hammond who?
Hammond eggs.

What did the cook name his son?
Stew.

What's a firefighter's favourite drink?
Water.

Monster School pupil: I don't like my granny.
Teacher: Have you tried her with salt and pepper?

Pardon?

What has ears but can't hear a thing?
A cornfield.

What is the most dangerous vegetable to have on a boat?
A leek.

What do you call a cow with no legs?
Ground beef.

What do you give to a sick lemon?
Lemon aid.

"Waiter! Waiter! What is this fly doing in my soup?"
"Looks like the backstroke, sir."

Knock Knock!
Who's there?
Ice cream.
Ice cream who?
Ice cream and ice cream until you open the door!

What do you call two banana peels?
A pair of slippers.

Why is a tomato round and red?
Because if it was long and green it would be a cucumber.

What's a ghost's favourite pasta?
Spookghetti.

Why did the biscuit go to the hospital?
He felt crummy.

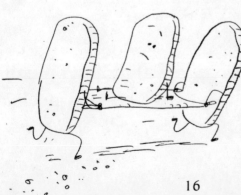

What chocolate bar lives in outer space?
The Milky Way.

How can you tell if an apple is organic?
Look for a healthy worm.

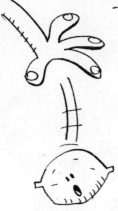

How do you make a lemon drop?
Let go of it.

What's in a piano teacher's favourite sandwich?
Tuna.

What can a whole orange do that half an orange can't?
Look round.

Why are cooks cruel?
Because they beat eggs and whip cream.

"Waiter! Waiter! There's a fly in my soup."
"Don't worry, sir. The spider on the roll will eat it."

What did the priest say to the friar who was always eating bananas?
"Stop being such a monk-ey."

What's a snowman's favourite cereal?
Frosted flakes.

What's the best day to eat fish and chips?
Fry-day.

When do you stop at green and go at red?
When you're eating watermelon.

Where do cucumbers go for a drink?
The salad bar.

What do you call a plum that likes to work on pipes?
A plum-er.

How do you fix a cracked pumpkin?
With a pumpkin patch.

What do you call artificial spaghetti?
Mockaroni.

What happens when you sit on a grape?
It gives a little whine.

What's the difference between roast beef and pea soup?
Anyone can roast beef.

How do you tease fruit?
Banananananana!

Why were the tomatoes red?
Because the lettuce told them rude stories.

What type of fruit steals honey?
Pooh Pear.

How did the butcher introduce his wife?
"Meat Patty."

What's a sea monster's favourite meal?
Fish and ships.

Knock Knock!
Who's there?
Ketchup.
Ketchup who?
Ketchup and I'll tell you!

What's yellow, brown and hairy?
Cheese on toast dropped on the carpet.

How do you make
a strawberry
shake?
*Take it to a
scary movie.*

What do peases,
beanses and
soupses come in?
Kansas.

What did the macaroni
say to the tomato?
*"Don't get saucy
with me."*

Why did the monster have a terrible tummy ache?
It had eaten somebody who disagreed with him.

CLiCK

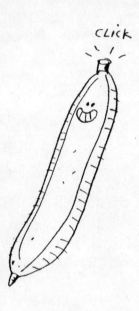

What is yellow and goes click, click?
A ballpoint banana.

How did Ronald McDonald celebrate his engagement?
He gave his girlfriend an onion ring.

Why did the baby strawberry cry?
Because his parents were in a jam.

What kind of lettuce did they serve on the *Titanic*?
Iceberg.

What type of cheese do dogs like on their pizza?
Mutts-erella.

How did the farmer mend his jeans?
With cabbage patches.

What kind of egg did the bad chicken lay?
A devilled egg.

What did the sausage say as it was about to be put on a skewer?
"Oh spear me, spear me!"

What fruit was a great conqueror?
Alexander the Grape.

What did the monster say when he saw a train packed full of people?
"Oh good, a chew-chew train."

Why did the turkey cross the road?
To prove he wasn't chicken.

What is brown, hairy and wears sunglasses?
A coconut on holiday.

What's the best month to eat toast?
Jam-uary.

What did the teddy bear say when he was offered dessert?
"No thanks, I'm stuffed."

**How do you make
a milkshake?**
*Creep up behind a
cow and say "BOO"!*

Why don't they serve chocolate in prison?
Because it makes people break out.

**Why did the worker at
the orange juice
factory lose his job?**
He couldn't concentrate.

**What do you eat at
a church supper?**
Hymn-burgers.

**What is green with
red spots?**
*A cabbage with
measles.*

Knock Knock!
Who's there?
Honeydew.
Honeydew who?
**Honeydew you
love me?**

**What kind of drink
never runs out?**
Infini-tea.

**Where was the first
doughnut made?**
In Grease.

**What do you get if
you eat too much
dessert?**
A stomach-cake.

Why did the orange stop rolling down the hill?
Because it ran out of juice.

What's a police officer's favourite lunch?
A club sandwich.

What did the mother biscuit say when her baby got run over?
"Oh, crumbs!"

If a carrot and a cabbage ran a race, who would win?
The cabbage, because it is always a head.

What did the pork chop say to the steak?
"Nice to meat you."

Why did the tomato blush?
Because it saw the salad dressing.

What's yellow and dangerous?
Shark-infested custard.

Why did the skeleton go to the barbecue?
He needed some spare ribs.

What did the mother ghost tell the baby ghost when he ate too fast?
"Stop goblin your food!"

What goes up a fruit and comes down a vegetable?
A tomato – throw it up and it comes down as squash.

Why can't you tell secrets in a vegetable garden?
The corn has ears and the potatoes have eyes.

Knock Knock!
Who's there?
Cash.
Cash who?
I knew you were a nut.

Diner: What's the difference between the white plate special and the brown plate special?

Waiter: The white plate special costs a lot more.

Diner: But is the food any different?

Waiter: Not usually, it's just that it'll be on a clean plate.

Knock Knock!
Who's there?
Kareem.
Kareem who?
Kareem tastes good in coffee.

Monster School pupil: What are we cooking for lunch today?

Monster School teacher: Shut up and get back in the oven.

What's worse than finding a slug in your salad?

Finding half a slug!

An old man and a young man worked next to each other in an office. The young man had noticed that the older man always seemed to have a jar of peanuts on his desk. The young man loved peanuts. One day when the older man was away from his desk, the young man couldn't resist and went to the jar and ate nearly all of the peanuts.

When the old man returned, the young man felt guilty and confessed to eating the peanuts.

The old man replied, "That's OK. Since I lost my teeth all I can do is suck the chocolate off the peanut M&Ms."

What do monsters eat for breakfast?
Dreaded wheat.

What did the hamburger name his daughter?
Patty.

What do you get if you cross a birthday cake with a can of baked beans?
A cake that blows out its own candles.

A man walked into a doctor's office. He had a cucumber up his nose, a carrot in his left ear and a banana in his right ear.

"What's the matter with me?" he asked the doctor.

The doctor replied, "You're not eating properly."

What do you get if you eat Christmas decorations? *Tinselitis.*

What's in an astronaut's favourite sandwich?
Launch meat.

What do sunbathers eat for breakfast?
Toast and eggs sunny side up.

What did the baby corn say to the mama corn?
"Where is pop corn?"

What do you get
when you cross a
witch with ice cubes?
A cold spell.

How do you make
pies sneaky?
*Add an "s" and
turn them
into spies.*

How do you
scramble eggs?
G-e-s-g.

Why couldn't the sesame seed leave the casino?
Because he was on a roll.

Why did the student eat his homework?
The teacher told him it was a piece of cake.

What's the best day to eat frozen food?
Thaws-day.

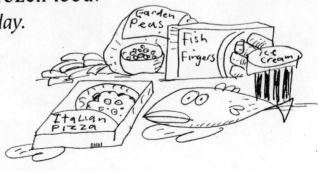

"Waiter! Waiter! There's a fly in my soup!"
"That's not a fly, sir, it's the chef. The last customer was a magician."

What do you have when 324 blueberries try to get through the same door?
Blueberry jam.

Why do fish avoid computers?
So they don't get caught in the Internet.

How can you tell if an elephant has been in your refrigerator?
Footprints in the butter.

I trained my dog not to beg at the table.
How did you do that?
I let him taste my cooking.

Why did the baby biscuit cry?
Because his mummy was a wafer so long.

What do you get when you put three ducks in a box?
A box of quackers.

"Waiter! Waiter! There's a worm on my plate!"
"That's no worm, sir, it's your sausage."

Table for one

What does the richest person in the world make for dinner every night?
Reservations.

Knock Knock!
Who's there?
Emil.
Emil who?
**Emil sounds good,
I'm hungry!**

**Why did the man
stare at the carton
of orange juice?**
*Because it said
"concentrate".*

**How does the
man in the moon
eat his food?**
In satellite dishes.

Monster Mash by T. Rex

COOKING FOR CROWDS by Howard Mennymore

BREAKFAST IS READY by Chris P. Bacon

Fast Food by Speedy Gonzalez

Giant Burgers by Big Mac

LEFTOVERS by Bubble and Squeak

MORE Leftovers by Bitson Peeces

Casserole Cooking by Stew Pot

Best Barbecues by Sunny Jim

FAIRY CAKES by Tinkerbell

What kind of witch likes cheese and ham?
A sandwich.

Where did the spaghetti go to dance?
The meat ball.

What's the heaviest noodle in the world?
A won-ton noodle.

**How do you make
a monster stew?**
*Keep it waiting for
two hours.*

**"Waiter! Waiter!
This food tastes
kind of funny."**
*"Then why aren't
you laughing?"*

**How can you stop
fish from going bad
on Mondays?**
Eat it on a Sunday.

**What do you get
when you cross fruit
with a necklace?**
A food chain.

How can you get breakfast in bed?
Sleep in the kitchen.

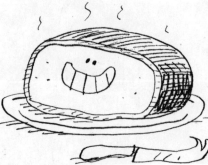

**What cheese is
made backwards?**
Edam.

What kind of nut always seems to have a cold?
Cashews.

Where's the best place to see a man-eating fish?
A seafood restaurant.

Knock Knock!
Who's there?
Duncan.
Duncan who?
Duncan biscuits in cocoa is yummy.

How do you help a
hungry cannibal?
Give him a hand.

"Waiter! Waiter!
This food is awful.
Bring me the
manager."
*"He won't taste any
better, sir."*

Why did the
doughnut go
to the dentist?
*It needed a
chocolate filling.*

Why did the chicken join the marching band?
Because he had two drumsticks.

How do birds eat leftovers?
Wormed up.

What's a monster's favourite lunch?
Baked beings.

**What do elves make
sandwiches with?**
Shortbread.

**Why did the ice cream
take karate lessons?**
It was tired of getting licked.

**What table can
you eat?**
A vege-table.

Why did the raisin go out with the prune? *Because she couldn't find a date.*

Why are eggs such losers? *Because they are always beaten.*

"Waiter! Waiter! Do you serve crabs here?" *"Yes, sir. We'll serve just about anybody."*

**What vitamin
helps you to see?**
Vitamin C.

**What food stays
hot when you
put it in the
refrigerator?**
Salsa.

Knock Knock!
Who's there?
Olive.
Olive who?
Olive you!

Why did the boy throw butter out the window?
He wanted to see a butterfly.

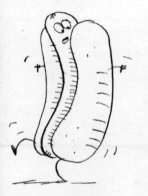

How do you make a hot dog stand?
Steal its chair.

What are the two things you can't have for breakfast?
Lunch and dinner.

**What do you feed
an invisible cat?**
Evaporated milk.

**What do vampires
like to drink?**
A Bloody Mary.

**How many
peas are there
in a pint?**
*There's one "p"
in a pint.*

**"Waiter! Waiter!
There's a fly in my soup."**
*"Sorry, sir, it should
have been in your roll."*

**Why doesn't the
corn like the
farmer?**
*Because he picks
its ears.*

**How do hens
encourage their
sports teams?**
They egg them on!

What do you get from a pampered cow?
Spoiled milk.

Why did the burglar rob the bakery?
He needed the dough.

Why did the girl nibble on her calendar?
She wanted a sundae.